ARIANA GRANDE
BREAK FREE

Katy Sprinkel

30 YEARS
TRIUMPH BOOKS

This book is available in quantity at special discounts for your group or organization. For further information, contact:

Triumph Books LLC
814 North Franklin Street
Chicago, Illinois 60610
(312) 337-0747
www.triumphbooks.com

Printed in U.S.A.

ISBN: 978-1-62937-719-3

Content written, developed, and packaged by
    Katy Sprinkel
Edited by Laine Morreau
Design and page production by Patricia Frey
Cover design by Preston Pisellini

Photographs by Getty Images

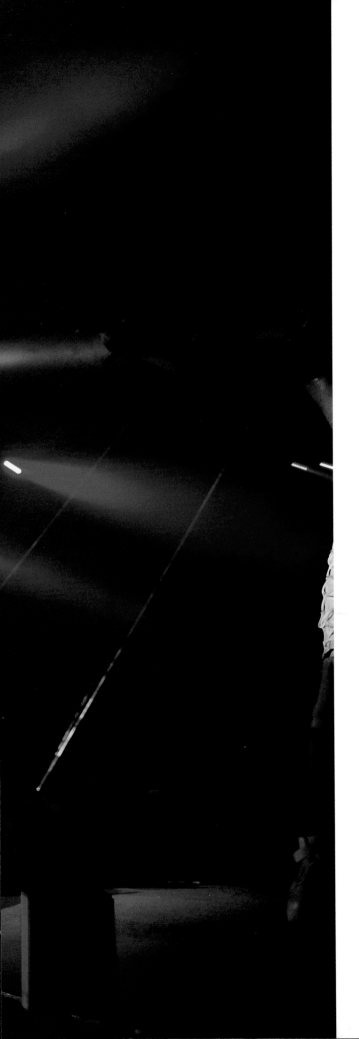

CONTENTS

{1}

SUCCESSFUL

She's fearless. She's frank. She's an artist at the top of her game. And she's just getting started!

These days, Ariana Grande is hitting all the high notes. Her fourth studio album, *Sweetener*, picked up two Grammy nominations, including Best Pop Vocal Album. She's the only artist ever to have the lead single from each of her first five albums debut in the top 10 of the Billboard Hot 100, and the first female artist in three years to have a single debut at No. 1 on the Hot 100.

Fans have been packing stadiums around the world to see her perform, and her upcoming 65-city world tour in support of not one but two albums in *Thank U, Next* and *Sweetener* has already sold out in multiple cities months in advance.

She's a social media powerhouse, with the third-most followers of *any* Instagrammer and the 11th-most of all Twitter users. Her online engagement with fans is next-level;

{ *55 million* }

Ari's video for "Thank U, Next" not only surpassed but *obliterated* YouTube Premieres records, capturing 55 million views in its first 24 hours alone (dethroning K-pop superstars BTS and their formidable ARMY of fans for good measure)! The hotly anticipated music video sees Ari channel the heroines of some of the most indelible comedies of the early aughts—*Mean Girls, Legally Blonde, 13 Going on 30*, and *Bring It On*.

Accepting 2018 Woman of the Year honors from Billboard.

At Coachella in 2018. Little did she know she'd be headlining the whole shebang the following year.

she regularly replies to fans via social media and tantalizes them with hints and details about every move she makes with her music and beyond. Her devoted legion of fans, the self-dubbed Arianators, are a force to be reckoned with. Just recently, they helped Ariana reach a huge milestone, making her "Thank U, Next" video the most watched YouTube video in a single day. Then her "7 Rings" broke Spotify's single-day listening record with almost 15 million streams in its first 24 hours (4 million more than the previous record holder).

Her nothing-is-off-limits songwriting also resonates with fans, who feel they know the artist's innermost thoughts and feelings. She's penned massive hits about everything from self-love ("Thank U, Next") and female empowerment ("God Is a Woman") to some very NSFW topics.

And then there's her voice. Undeniably, she has one of the most incredible voices in music, and many have tapped her as the heir apparent to powerhouse vocalists such as Mariah Carey, Celine Dion, and Whitney Houston. Make no mistake about it—Ari has the chops of those singers; she has a four-octave range that rivals any of the aforementioned legends. Presently, she seems poised to take over the mantle held by modern-day divas Taylor Swift, Katy Perry, and Beyoncé… if she hasn't already.

It was hard to go anywhere in 2018 without hearing her name. She was the object of intense tabloid scrutiny the instant her relationship with comedian Pete Davidson turned Instagram-official. (If you had a pulse during late 2018, you know how that one turned out.) She lost her ex-boyfriend and close friend Mac Miller to an accidental overdose in October, while engaged to Davidson. She was also very frank about the fact that she is still reeling from PTSD from the 2017 attack at her concert in Manchester, England, that left 22 fans dead and hundreds more injured.

All told, it was a tumultuous year for the singer, to put it mildly. Accepting Billboard Woman of the Year honors in November 2018, she spoke candidly to the audience about all of her recent ups and downs. "This has been one of the best years in my career and one of…the worst years in my life," she said, holding back tears. "I'm just saying that because I feel like a lot of people would look at

> "I feel like I've only scratched the surface of the artist I can be, and I just want to keep growing and practicing and getting better. I never want to get lazy."
> —to *Billboard*

The press' scrutiny of Ari and Pete Davidson during their engagement was intense.

At the Grammys
in 2014.

someone in my position…and think, you know, 'She's really got [it] together.'… I just want to say if you're someone out there who has no idea what this next chapter is going to bring, you're not alone."

The speech was typical Ari, whose candor is on permanent display in her music, on her socials, and in interviews. "If I'm going to be a role model, the last thing I should be is perfect, because that's not realistic," she told the BBC. "As long as I'm honest and genuine and I share with my fans my truest self, that's the best that I can do, because that's allowing them to do the same thing."

Her relatability, sheer talent, indefatigable work ethic, and refusal to be categorized are just a few of the reasons Arianators the world wide are singing her praises. And she's only getting started! ◆

Celebrating her win for Favorite Female Artist at the 2015 American Music Awards.

{2}

REMEMBER

Playing Snow White onstage in 2012.

It was a sunny summer day in Boca Raton, Florida, when Edward Butera and Joan Grande-Butera welcomed their baby girl into the world, joining half-brother Frankie, 10 years her senior.

In those early years, the Grande-Butera household was a happy home filled with music, love, and laughter. "My family was the stereotypical poker-playing, loud, friendly, food-shoving, loving Italian family," Ariana told *Complex* magazine. And although the name Ariana, meaning "holy one," might sound like a nod to the family's Roman Catholic faith, Edward and Joan were actually inspired by quite a different source. The name was taken from Princess Oriana, a character in the classic *Felix the Cat* cartoons of the early 20th century.

It was Ari's mother who was especially fond of classic Hollywood, and she made sure her daughter got exposure to the great films. This also extended to music, and Joan peppered young Ariana's musical education with some of the all-time great voices, including the inimitable Judy Garland. "Every day my mom and I would watch a different Judy Garland

VHS," Ari told *Billboard* in 2013. "I love how she tells a story when she sings. It was just about her voice and the words she was singing–no strings attached or silly hair or costumes, just a woman singing her heart out."

Joan has always been a role model for her daughter. She started her own company, which produces marine communication equipment, when she was eight months pregnant with Ariana, and still serves as its CEO to this day. Part of her vision

{ *Say What?* }

Turns out you've been pronouncing Ariana's last name wrong all this time. Thought it was GRAHN-day, like your Starbucks order? Nope, it's actually GRAN-dee—it rhymes with *candy*! Maybe *that's* why she named her fourth album *Sweetener*...

was to create a company that would fulfill the needs of working mothers like herself. "I built this building with a day-care area. I actually had it certified," Joan told *ELLE* magazine. "Employees brought their children, and Ariana was here almost every day."

But the positive female influence in Ari's life doesn't stop with her mother. The singer, who so vigorously celebrates female empowerment, comes from a long line of strong, empowered women! Her grandmother–Nonna, as she's known to Arianators the world over–is whip-smart, hilarious, and unapologetic. (Sound familiar?) And Ari's late aunt Judy was a Pulitzer Prize–nominated journalist and all-around glass-ceiling shatterer. The singer describes Judy and Joan as "through-and-through feminist queens."

Armed with Grande confidence and strength, Ari was poised for the spotlight from the start. And as far back as she can remember, she loved to perform. "I was always running around the house in

Joan joins Ari in celebrating the debut of her first fragrance.

costume and makeup. I was a different character every single day," she told Scholastic. And she was always singing. "We [were] running around the house screaming musicals, constantly singing songs from *Rent* and *Wicked*," big brother Frankie recalled to *Attitude* magazine. "There [was] always a performance going on in our house."

Singing was undoubtedly Ariana's greatest source of happiness, and she knew she had found her calling early on. "When I was six years old, I just kind of decided [singing is] what I'm going to do with my life, period," she told *Billboard* in 2018. "I manifested it. I knew I would. There was never really a doubt in my mind."

Sam & Cat costars Ari and Jennette McCurdy present at the 2013 Kids' Choice Awards.

She started doing community theater and landed the plum title role in *Annie* at age eight. Parents were not allowed to attend rehearsals unless they were in the show, so her mom auditioned so she could be there alongside her daughter. "[It] was the funniest thing that's ever happened in the history of the world, because my mom is a CEO, she has her own companies, her own full schedule," Ariana told the *Daily Telegraph*. "She was Daddy Warbucks' maid.… She had to wear a French maid's outfit and use a broom. She was like, 'I have no idea what I'm doing right now… but anything for my daughter.'"

Ari sports her natural hair during an appearance with the cast of *13* in 2008.

Around the same time, Ariana had her first brush with stardom when she performed karaoke on a cruise ship in front of a huge crowd that just happened to include the famous pop star Gloria Estefan. Apparently Estefan was so impressed with Ari's singing that she came over after the performance to offer her some words of encouragement. "I literally went up to her and told her and her mom, 'I don't know if you plan on doing this, but this is what you need to be doing because you are an amazing singer,'" Estefan told the *Daily News*. "It was amazing."

Sadly, it was also around this time that Ariana's parents divorced. "That was very hard," Ari told the *Daily Telegraph*. "Being in the middle of it was so stressful.

And of course being made up of both of them—I was like, 'Hey, if they both dislike each other's attributes so much, what am I to like about [myself]?'… It was traumatic."

Her mother and Nonna and the rest of the family kept her steady during that difficult period—during which she became estranged from her father—and music gave her a vehicle for channeling difficult emotions. Within a few years, she was auditioning on bigger stages. She landed the role of Charlotte in the Broadway musical *13* at age 15, winning a National Youth Theatre Association Award for her performance. Suddenly, she was in the national spotlight. By then, Ariana had quit school to pursue a career in

{ *Did You Know?* }

Despite her incredible range and control, Ariana never received any formal vocal training.

acting and music. And even though she was laser-focused on her goal, it wasn't without trepidation that she made such a big move.

Nickelodeon took notice of Ari in *13*, and in 2009 she was cast on *Victorious* as Cat Valentine, the sweet, energetic, fire-engine-red-haired bubblehead denizen of Hollywood Arts High School. From there, her showbiz career took off in earnest. As luck would have it, producers

"When I was six years old, I just kind of decided [singing is] what I'm going to do with my life, period."
—to *Billboard*

Girls' night out with Nonna at the 2014 VMAs.

"I grew up with a...brother whose every move
I would emulate. I idolized him. Everything
Frankie did, I would do."—to *Billboard* in 2018

also tapped her *13* castmate (and Lindsay Lohan dead ringer) Elizabeth Gillies for the show. The two have remained close friends for more than a decade.

Cat was a longtime fan favorite, and the network ultimately decided to spin off Cat from *Victorious* and Jennette McCurdy's Sam Puckett from *iCarly* to create the series *Sam & Cat*. The show followed the comic adventures—more often misadventures—of the titular characters and their Super Rockin' Fun Time Babysitting Service. The show was a hit for Nick, but it was abruptly canceled after 36 episodes amid swirling rumors of rivalries, scandal (in the form of leaked photos of McCurdy), and diva-like clashes between its two principal stars.

Ari stayed above the fray, posting a heartfelt message to her fans on Twitter after news of the cancellation broke, writing in part: "I will always hold Cat near and dear to my heart…. I think a lot of people could take a page out of her book…… she wouldn't judge anybody by

Sporting her Cat Valentine locks in 2010.

their appearance…. she believed the best in people…. she wasn't afraid of anything or anybody…. she never let people's judgements hold her back from doing what she wanted, acting how she wanted, dressing how she wanted…[dyeing] her hair however she wanted… she never held back her enthusiasm or joy for fear of appearing some sort of way or for fear of jinxing the good that is real (which is something I personally do all the time but

{Vital Stats }

Full name: Ariana Joan Grande-Butera

Birthday: June 26, 1993

Astrological sign: Cancer

Birthplace: Boca Raton, Florida

Parents: Edward Butera and Joan Grande

Sibling: Half-brother Frankie Grande

Other family members: Her pets (nine dogs and a pig at last count)

Heritage: Italian-American

Nicknames: Ari, Riri, Little Red (a throwback to her Cat Valentine days)

Height: Five foot zero

Eye color: Brown

Early musical influences: India.Arie, Mariah Carey, Whitney Houston, Imogen Heap

First idol: Judy Garland

First concert: Katy Perry (flash forward a few years: Perry said Ariana has "the best female vocal in pop music today")

First steady gig: *13* on Broadway

Favorite colors: periwinkle, lavender, pale pink, marshmallow white

Favorite holiday: Halloween

Favorite flicks: Scary movies

Favorite books: *Lord of the Rings* and the Harry Potter series

Place she most wants to be: In the studio

Can't live without: Her family and her pets

Can't live with: Shellfish, bananas, and cats—she's allergic!

Favorite foods: Daikon, adzuki beans, lotus, blueberries (she is a vegan)

Secret talent: She's an excellent impressionist

I wish I could shake that and celebrate every little thing like she does).

"One of my favorite things about Cat was that she never lost her sense of wonder. As we grow up we become more and more jaded and fearful of how we come across. We hold back a little more, protect ourselves a little more and although Cat goes through the same ridicule as anybody else does growing up, she never changed or lost her childlike wonder. To me that's the bravest, most special thing about her. She actually reminds me a lot of [my half-brother] Frankie in that way.

"So I know a lot of people will think this is a lot for some 'dumb' kids show character.... but to me she is actually a lot smarter, stronger and braver than all the rest of us."

Meanwhile, Ariana's music career was about to take off. She'd been working on her debut album on and off for the better part of three years while shooting

Victorious and *Sam & Cat*. Finally, with the cancellation of the latter—and armed with the lessons she'd learned from her time playing Cat Valentine—she was ready to take center stage with her music career. ◆

Visiting a young patient at St. Jude Children's Research Hospital in 2011.

{3}

SIDE TO SIDE

Performing "Problem" with Iggy Azalea at the 2014 Billboard Music Awards.

Pop music is a hugely collaborative art form, and Ari has worked side *by* side with some of the biggest names in the industry over the course of her career so far, both onstage and behind the scenes.

Ariana started releasing music while she was still a budding talent at Nick. It was a great opportunity to jump-start her recording career, but Ari was conflicted. She released her debut single, the bubble-gum anthem to optimism "Put Your Hearts Up," in 2013, but it failed to chart. (She later disavowed the single, even removing it from her Vevo page. "I feel like [it] would have been Cat's single. I really wanted to do music, but I couldn't wait. So I was stuck in this weird world where it was like 'I'm Cat, but I'm…me,'" she told *Zach Sang and the Gang* in 2015.)

It wasn't until she left television and the role of Cat Valentine behind that Ari felt comfortable showing her fans who she really was as an artist and a person. She heralded this arrival with the release of her 2013 album, *Yours Truly*, which had been a work in progress for years— she started working on it while still on *Victorious*. "Hearts Up" didn't make the final cut for the album, as Ari felt it was

Released September 3, 2013

Inside the Track: "Popular Song" (feat. Mika)

British artist Mika tapped *Wicked* superfan Ari to join him on a version of the Broadway song.

"inauthentic," and authenticity was of the utmost importance to her by that time. As she focused on revealing her true self, part of that process meant distinguishing herself from the naïve, optimistic Cat, projecting a little more maturity and chipping away at that goody-two-shoes image.

Fittingly, given Ari's efforts to distance herself from her former image, the lead single from *Yours Truly*, "The Way," sidesteps kiddie pop, and Mac Miller lends a gritty edge to the track, spitting lyrics like "You're a princess in the public but a freak when it's time." It's a throwback to radio-friendly '90s R&B,

begging comparisons to vocally adroit divas such as Mariah Carey. Indeed, *Rolling Stone* called the single "flirty rather than freaky," adding "her Mariah-esque vocals verge on ecstatic." MTV was rapturous, proclaiming her "the hottest pop newcomer in the game." The single debuted in the Billboard top 10 and went on to be certified platinum. The entire album was a commercial success—debuting at No. 1 on the Billboard 200 and earning platinum certification—and a critical triumph too. *Pitchfork* called it "not your typical pop album" with "ludicrously powerful" vocals.

Aside from Mac Miller, *Yours Truly* brought in more collaborative firepower in Nathan Sykes (the Wanted), Big Sean, and Mika on vocals and producers Babyface and Harmony Samuels behind the scenes. It was also Ari's first of many collaborations with producer Tommy Brown ("Honeymoon Avenue," "Daydreamin'"). Also notably, Ari paired up on the record with songwriter and future bestie Victoria Monét, who wrote

{ *Did You Know?* }

Aside from her major albums, Ari has also released two Christmas EPs: *Christmas Kisses* (2013) and *Christmas & Chill* (2015).

"Sisters" Ari and Nicki Minaj work it out at the 2016 MTV VMAs.

ARTIST OF THE YEAR
ARIANA GRANDE

Accepting the award for Artist of the Year at the 2016 AMAs.

two tracks on the debut ("Honeymoon Avenue" and "Daydreamin'"). The two have gone on to work together on every album since then and are very close friends.

In August 2014 Ari released her next album, *My Everything*, which shot immediately to the top of the charts. It was the second straight No. 1 debut—two in less than a year's time (not bad, considering it took more than three years to complete *Yours Truly*). The A.V. Club called it "a slick throwback to melodramatic '80s and '90s pop" that "further establishes Grande as a consummate performer and vocal interpreter," and *Rolling Stone* heralded it as "a confident, intelligent, brazen pop statement, mixing bubblegum diva vocals with EDM break beats."

It was also a step further in her maturity, and she pushed the boundaries of her lyrical content into hot and heavy territory while exploring a more expansive sound. She did so with the

{ My Everything }

Released August 25, 2014

Inside the Track: "Break Your Heart Right Back" (feat. Childish Gambino)

Ari and Childish Gambino are topliners at Coachella. Is it too much to ask for a "Break Your Heart Right Back" duet?

help of some huge names in hip-hop and R&B—the likes of The Weeknd, Childish Gambino, Iggy Azalea, Zedd, A$AP Ferg, and Big Sean. She was "an innocent newcomer no more," wrote the *Los Angeles Times* in its review of the record.

My Everything also marked the first of many collaborations with producer and

Swedish hitmaker Max Martin. He cowrote and produced four songs on the album, including the defiant kiss-off to an ex, "Problem," with a little help from Iggy Azalea. The single debuted at No. 3 on the Hot 100, making it remarkably the fifth-highest debut for a female artist in the chart's history and Ari's highest-charting single to date. "Break Free," her collaboration with Zedd, was another departure for Ari. (It was "fantastic and super-experimental for me," she told *Billboard*. "I never thought I'd do an EDM song, but that was an eye-opening experience, and now all I want to do is dance.") And if "The Way" had

Jessie J and Ari perform their smash "Bang Bang" at the iHeart Radio 2014 Jingle Ball.

been coquettish, "Love Me Harder" left little to the imagination. Teaming up with The Weeknd, the unlikely pairing made for musical magic. *Billboard* wrote, "The driving guitar riff in the chorus is delicious '80s cheese, and The Weeknd's ultra-sincere crooning works well while serving as callbacks to Grande's demands for romantic satisfaction."

Meanwhile, Republic Records labelmates Ari, Jessie J, and Nicki Minaj formed a triple threat with the much-anticipated "Bang Bang," which was the lead single of Jessie J's *Sweet Talker*. The sizzling track became one of the hottest songs of the summer, with Ari belting out such come-hither lyrics as "See, anybody could be good to you / You need a bad girl to blow your mind." Incredibly, Ariana achieved *three* songs in the Billboard top 10 simultaneously with that release (coupled with "Problem" and "Break Free" off *My Everything*). The song was added to the deluxe edition of *My Everything* following that success.

Ari released *Dangerous Woman* in 2016, and by that point, she was a far cry from the Pollyanna who had urged listeners to put their hearts up to heal the world. This dangerous woman was all grown up, and the music signaled her independence, as lyrics like "I used to let some people tell

{ *Dangerous Woman* }

DANGEROUS WOMAN

Released May 20, 2016

Inside the Track: "Moonlight"

Originally intended to be the title and lead single of the album, Ariana decided to go with something more "empowering." Speaking to *Billboard*, she said, "To me, a dangerous woman is someone who's not afraid to take a stand, be herself and to be honest."

When Madonna calls, you answer. Ari performing at Madonna Presents an Evening of Music, Art, Mischief and Performance to Benefit Raising Malawi.

me how to live and what to be…. But if I can't be me, [what's] the point?" make unmistakably clear. It seemed she was finally comfortable in her own skin.

Entertainment Weekly raved about *Dangerous Woman* and its unique sense of purpose. "[Grande has] something meaningful to say with that jaw-dropping voice—one of the most exquisite in pop today," wrote critic Nolan Feeney. "Ex–child stars, looking to shed G-rated images, tend to stop at F-bombs and sex boasts, yet this former Nickelodeon idol uses her platform to challenge the expectations facing young female celebrities." In *Woman*, she takes down everyone from social media slut-shamers to misogynistic interviewers to the image-focused record industry itself.

The title single debuted at No. 10 on the Billboard charts, making Ari the only artist ever to score top 10 hits with the lead single on her or his first three albums. She followed "Dangerous Woman" with "Into You" and "Side to Side"—the latter yet another Nicki Minaj collaboration—and both singles emerged as some of her highest-charting songs to date. And while she enlisted more heavy hitters as guest stars on the album—including the likes of Missy Elliott and Macy Gray—this time around it was more about Ari's wide-ranging vocals.

Arianators thought she had hit the sweet spot with *Dangerous Woman*, and then came *Sweetener*. It was far and away Ari's biggest release. But more important, it was her best-received. *Rolling Stone* called it her "best album yet, and one of 2018's strongest pop releases to date." The *Guardian* hailed it as "a defiant record, chronicling both the difficulty and necessity of choosing to be happy."

She kept her Billboard winning streak going with the album's lead single, "No Tears Left to Cry," which again debuted in the chart's top 10. The song, in part an elegy to the victims of the 2017

Manchester bombing, was the first new music she'd released since the tragedy. It is a beautiful tribute to those lost and a stirring exhortation about moving on. She followed that up with the provocative (and some say Queen Bey–like) "God Is a Woman" and the confessional "Breathin."

{ *Sweetener* }

Released August 17, 2018

Inside the Track: "Get Well Soon"

Ari has described this track as "the grown-up honeymoon avenue," explaining it's "all the voices in my head talking to each other." The track ends with 40 seconds of silence, taking the run time to 5:22—the date of the Manchester attack.

Ari cowrote 10 of the 15 songs on the record, and it's clear that *Sweetener* was her most personal to date. And if that effort wasn't communicated clearly enough, even the video for "No Tears Left to Cry" finds her putting down the literal masks that she wears.

The record closes with "Get Well Soon," in which Ari tackles her struggles with anxiety head-on. Speaking to Troye Sivan in *Paper* magazine, she talked about the song's origins. "[Producer Pharrell Williams] kind of forced it out of me, because I was in a really bad place mentally. I've always had anxiety, I've had anxiety for years. But when I got home from [the Dangerous Woman] tour it reached a very different, intense peak. It became physical and I was not going out at all, and I felt like I was outside my body. I'd have these spells every now and then where I felt like I was having déjà vu, but like 24/7 for three months at a time. It was really weird, and all that was on my mind. [Pharrell] was like, 'You have to write about it. You need to make this into music and get this [stuff] out, and I promise it will heal you.' And it definitely helped."

Arianators have often celebrated their idol for her willingness to talk (and create music) about difficult subjects, not least of all her struggles with anxiety. It's one of many examples of Ari laying herself bare, and her emotional honesty resonates with listeners struggling with their own highs and lows, whether anxiety and depression or the sting of a breakup or the difficulty of being one's authentic self.

The tracks on *Sweetener* may have been a form of self-therapy for the artist, but they don't have anything on "Thank U, Next." The epic breakup anthem is actually the ultimate anti-breakup song—a bold declaration of self-love without recrimination. ("Plus, I met someone else / … her name is Ari / And I'm so good with that," she croons.)

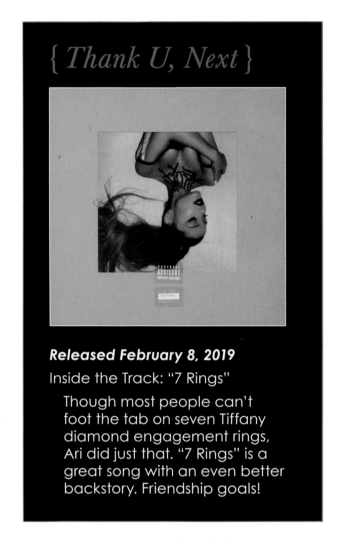

{ *Thank U, Next* }

Released February 8, 2019
Inside the Track: "7 Rings"
Though most people can't foot the tab on seven Tiffany diamond engagement rings, Ari did just that. "7 Rings" is a great song with an even better backstory. Friendship goals!

The single basically broke the Internet and primed the pump for her upcoming fifth album release. It's her most confessional album yet, written and produced in a short span of time alongside her closest friends ("made with tru [sic], deep friendship and love," as she told fans on Twitter). ◆

{4}

FOCUS

Ari's journey to superstardom has been meteoric, and it's 100 percent the result of laser-like focus. A big part of that journey has been the literal miles that she's traveled, when she's been able to connect with fans face-to-face.

Since she released her first album, *Yours Truly*, in 2013, she has headlined three major tours and played to hundreds of packed stadiums across the world.

Her first huge gig on the road was as an opening act for Justin Bieber—a fellow Scooter Braun artist and at the time *the* biggest pop star in the nation. The Biebs took Ari with him on a handful of 2013 dates during his Believe tour. "I can't get over how nice and warm and welcoming

his fans were to me.… It was a whirlwind. I loved it," she told *ELLE* at the time.

Of course, Arianators know what happened next. Flash forward fourteen months, and she was headlining her own arena tour. It didn't happen without a lot of preparation, perspiration, and determination. "That's the part of the American Dream that I think some people who really want to be recognized don't realize—how much work goes along with it," she told *Clash* magazine in 2014. "A lot of people just want to be famous. I never wanted that; I just wanted to make music."

Her longtime producer Tommy Brown acknowledged that women artists often have to work harder and are more dedicated than their male counterparts—a prime reason why he prefers working with women. And Ari, a self-confessed workaholic, has been successful precisely because she outworks *everybody*. "She leaves [the stage], kicks off her boots and

Opening for Bieber in 2013.

On top of the
world in 2014.

is like, 'Let's go to the studio.' And that's like whoa. I've never seen a guy do that," Brown told *Mitu*.

Indeed, Ari has long said that being in the studio is her absolute favorite part of the process, and she has increasingly asserted herself in that realm. She is a confident producer with mad skills in the booth and a keen instinct for what works and what doesn't. Creating music is also, quite simply, her happy place. When heartbreak came her way in late 2018, it was straight to the studio that she went. ("How do u think I survived the last 2/3 months?" she Instagrammed, calling making new music "my lifeline." The result was *Thank U, Next*.

Dropping a new album just months after another may not have been the plan from the beginning, but Ari relied on her own instincts when it comes to her fifth album. "I don't want to do what people tell me to do. I don't want to conform to the pop star agenda," she told *Billboard*. "I

want to do it on my own terms from now on. If I want to tour two albums at once, I'm going to tour two albums at once. If I want to drop a third album while I'm on tour [in 2019], I'll do that too!… I want to be able to do what is authentic and honest and natural. It's the only way that I've been able to survive."

> ## { *Did You Know?* }
>
> Before she was an actress, *This Is Us*'s Chrissy Metz was Ari's talent agent! Metz repped Ari's future *Hairspray Live!* costar and pal Dove Cameron too, and predicted the pair would be famous long before they were household names. "You know they're going to be stars when you meet them for the first time," she told *The Tonight Show Starring Jimmy Fallon*.

This also means controlling how and when her music gets out there, even if it's sometimes to others' chagrin. (Her manager, Scooter Braun, has said that he never knows when Ari is going to tease her fans with something top secret, undoing the careful plans of her team.) And when she tweets a snippet of lyrics or a shred of a track list or a behind-the-scenes photo, it does feel like she's genuinely excited to share the fruits of her labor.

Having fully taken control of her story, there is no aspect of her music and tour that she doesn't touch these days. "I run my show entirely from top to bottom," she told *Cosmopolitan* in 2018. "I realized how not okay I am with

{ *$71 million* }

In 77 dates across five continents, the Dangerous Woman tour grossed $71 million. Nearly 1 million people turned out to see Ari perform live on the tour!

putting everything in someone else's hands, because if I'm going to make art then I should care about how the art is going to be handled and how it's going to be represented. I have to think about everything, and I didn't realize it's a full-time job. Now, I'm very much in charge, and it feels amazing." ◆

{ "I don't want to do what people tell me to do. I don't want to conform to the pop star agenda." }

Ari takes center stage during a stop in Phoenix on the Dangerous Woman tour.

{ *Globe-Trotter* }

Looks like Ari's going to spend most of 2019 on the road. She kicks off her world tour in Upstate New York in March and winds it down seven months later in Switzerland. Where will *you* see Ari this year?

(Dates are according to arianagrande.com and are current as of the time of this writing.)

March 18
Albany, NY, USA
Times Union Center

March 20
Boston, MA, USA
TD Garden

March 22
Buffalo, NY, USA
KeyBank Center

March 25
Washington, DC, USA
Capitol One Arena

March 26
Philadelphia, PA, USA
Wells Fargo Center

March 28
Cleveland, OH, USA
Quicken Loans Arena

March 30
Uncasville, CT, USA
Mohegan Sun Arena

April 1
Montréal, Canada
Bell Centre

April 3
Toronto, Canada
Scotiabank Arena

April 5
Detroit, MI, USA
Little Caesars Arena

April 14
Indio, CA, USA
Coachella Valley Music and Arts Festival

April 21
Indio, CA, USA
Coachella Valley Music and Arts Festival

April 25
Edmonton, AB, Canada
Rogers Place

April 27
Vancouver, BC, Canada
Rogers Arena

April 30
Portland, OR, USA
Moda Center

May 2
San Jose, CA, USA
SAP Center

May 3
Sacramento, CA, USA
Golden 1 Center

May 6
Los Angeles, CA, USA
Staples Center

May 7
Los Angeles, CA, USA
Staples Center

May 10
Los Angeles, CA, USA
The Forum

May 11
Las Vegas, NV, USA
T-Mobile Arena

May 14
Phoenix, AZ, USA
Talking Stick Resort Arena

May 17
San Antonio, TX, USA
AT&T Center

May 19
Houston, TX, USA
Toyota Center

May 21
Dallas, TX, USA
American Airlines Center

May 23
Oklahoma City, OK, USA
Chesapeake Energy Arena

May 25
New Orleans, LA, USA
Smoothie King Center

May 28
Tampa, FL, USA
Amalie Arena

May 29
Orlando, FL, USA
Amway Center

May 31
Miami, FL, USA
American Airlines Arena

June 1
Miami, FL, USA
American Airlines Arena

June 4
Chicago, IL, USA
United Center

June 5
Chicago, IL, USA
United Center

June 7
Nashville, TN, USA
Bridgestone Arena

June 8
Atlanta, GA, USA
State Farm Arena

June 10
Charlotte, NC, USA
Spectrum Center

June 12
Pittsburgh, PA, USA
PPG Paints Arena

June 14
Brooklyn, NY, USA
Barclays Center

June 15
Brooklyn, NY, USA
Barclays Center

June 18
New York, NY, USA
Madison Square Garden

June 19
New York, NY, USA
Madison Square Garden

June 21
Washington, DC, USA
Capital One Arena

June 22
Boston, MA, USA
TD Garden

June 24
Philadelphia, PA, USA
Wells Fargo Center

June 26
Toronto, ON, Canada
Scotiabank Arena

June 29
Indianapolis, IN, USA
Bankers Life Fieldhouse

July 1
Columbus, OH, USA
The Schottenstein Center

July 5
Milwaukee, WI, USA
Fiserv Forum

July 6
St. Louis, MO, USA
Enterprise Center

July 8
St. Paul, MN, USA
Xcel Energy Center

July 11
Denver, CO, USA
Pepsi Center

July 13
Salt Lake City, UT, USA
Vivint Smart Home Arena

August 17
London, England
The O2 Arena

August 19
London, England
The O2 Arena

August 20
London, England
The O2 Arena

August 23
Amsterdam, Netherlands
Ziggo Dome

August 24
Amsterdam, Netherlands
Ziggo Dome

August 27
Paris, France
AccorHotels Arena

August 28
Paris, France
AccorHotels Arena

August 30
Antwerp, Belgium
Sportpaleis Antwerpen

September 1
Cologne, Germany
Lanxess Arena

September 3
Vienna, Austria
Stadthalle

September 5
Hamburg, Germany
Barclaycard Arena

September 8
Prague, Czech Republic
O2 arena

September 9
Krakow, Poland
Tauron Arena

September 11
Amsterdam, Netherlands
Ziggo Dome

September 14
Birmingham, England
Arena Birmingham

September 15
Birmingham, England
Arena Birmingham

September 17
Glasgow, Scotland
The SSE Hydro

September 19
Sheffield, England
FlyDSA Arena

September 22
Dublin, Ireland
3Arena

September 23
Dublin, Ireland
3Arena

October 1
Copenhagen, Denmark
Royal Arena

October 3
Oslo, Norway
Telenor Arena

October 5
Helsinki, Finland
Hartwall Arena

October 7
Stockholm, Sweden
Ericsson Globe

October 10
Berlin, Germany
Mercedes-Benz Arena

October 13
Zurich, Switzerland
Hallenstadion

{5}

DANGEROUS WOMAN

Performing at the March
for Our Lives in 2018.

Some celebrities are calculated and careful with what they say, for fear of alienating people in their fan base, but from the beginning Ari has never been shy when it comes to her opinions.

If there's a refrain you hear about Ari time and time again it's that she's real—full stop. One could argue that it's her honesty as a person and as a songwriter that has won over fans to begin with.

She may occasionally get into hot water for some of the things she says, but it is of the utmost importance to her that she speaks her mind, no filter. She's the first one to object if an interviewer gets out of line (check YouTube for supercuts of *that* magic) or not-so-gently nudge her followers on social media when they step out of line. Take her breakup with Pete Davidson, for instance. Immediately

following the broken engagement, some Arianators trolled the comedian. Ari swiftly shut that down ("Be gentler," she admonished). "I really don't endorse anything but forgiveness and positivity," she continued via her Instagram story. And she seems to embody that ethos through and through.

Fostering sensitivity and inclusivity among her online community is something she won't compromise on. "The most important thing is to have

{ *Fanchat* }

"Beyond grateful to ariana for helping me feel empowered and beautiful in my own skin. she's helped me through so much and made me feel more loved than i ever thought i could. i love you @arianagrande #SelfiesForAriana"

—@hersweeteners via Instagram

each other's backs," she told *Coveteur*. "When you see something or hear something that's upsetting, or someone says something that's upsetting, even if it's not to you, just say something and be there and support each other.... It's about the sisterhood. There's no competing in that. We have to lift each other up, not try and claw each other down."

She's also plugged in to what's happening in the world around her. She has been harshly critical of President Trump and his policies. "In tears" on Election Night, she railed against Trump and his politics of divisiveness. "Let's please be active and vocal every day toward making each other feel accepted and loved for our differences," she urged her Twitter followers. "Not just on election day. please. It's the only way we will be able to get through what could possibly be a very dark few years."

She rallied her fan base to get out there and vote. She's a gun-control advocate, a supporter of the Black Lives Matter movement, and an ardent feminist (from a long line of them, natch). She walked alongside her mother and Nonna at the Women's March, performed at the March for Our Lives following the devastating Parkland school shooting, and played the Concert for Charlottesville benefit after violent protests broke out in the Virginia city. Citing her fortitude, *Time* magazine put her on its cover as one of its "Next Generation Leaders" in 2018.

{ "Not everyone is going to agree with you, but that doesn't mean I'm just going to shut up and sing my songs." }

"Not everyone is going to agree with you," Ari told *ELLE* magazine, "but that doesn't mean I'm just going to shut up and sing my songs." She continued, "I'm also going to be a human being who cares about other human beings; to be an ally and use my privilege to help educate people." An artist's role is "not only to help people and comfort them but also [to] push people to think differently, raise questions, and push their boundaries mentally," she elaborated.

Ari encourages dialogue above all else, no matter how difficult it might be. "Everyone has to have uncomfortable conversations with their relatives," she said. "Instead of unfriending people on Facebook who share different political views, comment! Have a conversation! Try to spread the…light!"

One issue she is particularly vocal about is gay rights. "I was raised in a household where being gay was like, the most normal thing," she told Ryan Murphy in *V* magazine. "You know, my brother is

Ari performs at the Concert for Charlottesville in 2017.

Ari waves the flag for inclusivity.

gay, all of my best friends are gay. When my brother came out of the closet, it wasn't a big deal for my family. Even my grandpa, who is like, super old-school, was like, 'Good for you!'" She continued, "It's outrageous to me when I see people hate on someone because of their sexuality. I hate the intolerance. I hate the judgment. I hate it so much. Most of my favorite people in my life are gay. It's something I'm super passionate about, because whenever I would see my friends get bullied, or my brother get hurt for his sexuality, I would become a raging lunatic...because I just can't take it."

Frankie recalled the moment he came out to her to *Attitude*: "I came out to her when she was just 11 years old, and she said: 'Great, when do I get to meet your boyfriend?'" He continued, "She was raised in a family where gay was not only accepted, it was celebrated. The fact that some people are in families who throw them out because they're gay or they're being told they're wrong because of who they are, it's a tragedy, and both she and I feel it's our responsibility to educate those people and help them see that we're all the same."

Ari headlined New York City's Pride concert in 2015, just days after gay marriage was legalized by the US Supreme Court—where she issued an excoriating directive for the dissenting justices while onstage—and she penned an essay for *Billboard* in honor of Pride Month in 2018, writing in part, "Love is like music. It knows no boundaries and isn't exclusive to any one gender, sexuality, race, religion, age or creed. It's a freedom and a delicious luxury that all people should be able to sink into and enjoy every moment of." The magazine once even dubbed her "the gay icon of her generation."

For Arianators, their idol doesn't just talk the talk; she walks the walk. Go, girl! ◆

{ *Reading the Fine Print* }

Ari has never shied away from expressing a strong opinion. In the music video for "Thank U, Next," she displays a pretty topical one for the current political climate. In a *Legally Blonde*–inspired segment of the video, Ari, dressed up in her best Elle Woods attire, brushes up on a volume of *Immigration and Refugee Law and Policy*.

{*The Queen of Clapbacks*}

Lots of celebrities claim that they don't read comments on social media, but Ari sees it differently. She wants Arianators to be on the up and up, and she will straight-up call someone out for saying something inappropriate, whether it's an Internet troll or even a celebrity (here's looking at you, Piers Morgan…and you, Bette Midler…and you too, Kanye West). It's one of the things Arianators can count on her for. Here is just a sampling of some of her most epic clapbacks.

That time someone accused her of being too provocative in the "Dangerous Woman" video…

When will people stop being offended by women showing skin / expressing sexuality? Men take their shirts off / express their sexuality on stage, in videos, on Instagram, anywhere they want to…all. the. time. The double standard is boring and exhausting…. Woman [sic] can love their bodies too!

That time people accused her and Nicki Minaj of being rivals because they had the same record release date…

jesus is this what's going on today? imma jus stop logging in at all lmfao. that's my…sister. she's clearing a sample. buy and stream queen & sweetener aug 17 bye. these numbers don't mean as much to the artist as they do to y'all. jus want y'all to listen to the project.

That time someone accused her of using sex to sell records…

seeing a lot of "but look how you portray yourself in videos and in your music! you're so sexual!" Expressing sexuality in art is not an invitation for disrespect!!! Just like wearing a short skirt is not asking for assault. Women's choice. Love our bodies, our clothing, our music, our personalities…… sexy, flirty, fun. it is not. an open. invitation.

That time she went to Twitter after a Mac Miller fan complimented him on "hitting that"…

This may not seem like a big deal to some of you but I felt sick and objectified…. Things like this happen all the time and are the kinds of moments that contribute to women's sense of fear and inadequacy. I am not a piece of meat that a man gets to utilize for his pleasure. I'm an adult human being in a relationship with a man who treats me with love and respect. It hurts my heart that so many young people are so comfortable enough using these phrases and objectifying women with such ease…. We need to share and be vocal when something makes us feel uncomfortable because if we don't, it will just continue.

That time a fan compared her body to Ariel Winter's…

Statements like this are not okay. About anyone!!! We live in a day and age where people make it IMPOSSIBLE for women, men, anyone to embrace themselves exactly how they are. Diversity is sexy! Loving yourself is sexy! You know what is NOT sexy? Misogyny, objectifying, labeling, comparing and body shaming!!!

That time someone blamed her for Mac Miller's DUI...
how absurd that you minimize female self-respect and self-worth by saying someone should stay in a toxic relationship because he wrote an album about them, which btw isn't the case.... I am not a babysitter or a mother and no woman should feel that they need to be. I have cared for him and tried to support his sobriety & prayed for his balance for years (and always will of course) but shaming / blaming women for a man's inability to keep his [stuff] together is a very major problem. Let's please stop doing that.

That time someone accused her of cheating on Mac Miller with Pete Davidson...
I didn't but go off. Can u like...go stan someone else. Ur boring.

That time someone accused Scooter Braun of engineering her engagement to Pete Davidson and Justin Bieber's engagement to Hailey Baldwin...
You do realize we are human beings who love and have lives....right....?

Do these two look like rivals?

and that scooter is a wonderful human being too who cares first n foremost ab our health and happiness? Love is lit.... I hope to god it happens to you too. U deserve it.

That time someone accused her of milking Mac Miller's death for publicity...
i pray you never have to deal with anything like this ever and i'm sending you peace and love.... some of the [stuff] i read on here makes me sick to my stomach. it scares me the way some people think and i don't like this world a lot of the time. if only we could be more compassionate and gentle with one another. that'd be sick.

{6}

RIGHT THERE

Ari brings her cousin Lani, Nonna, and her mother onstage at the end of her "God Is a Woman" performance at the 2018 VMAs.

There have been so many people who have been right there for Ariana during her long journey to superstardom.

That's especially true of 2018—Ariana called it the toughest year of her life—when she leaned on her squad like never before. This chapter is a who's who of Ariana's closest peeps and well-known friends for the uninitiated and Arianators alike.

Scootie Anderson and Mikey Foster: The duo known as Social House, a fellow Scooter Braun act, has already collaborated with Ari and will join her on her 2019 world tour.

Colleen Ballinger: Better known as YouTuber Miranda Sings, Ballinger is a pal from way back. (A very pregnant Ballinger appears in the video for "Thank U, Next," hilariously quipping that she

> "[Ari] is fierce, courageous, hilarious, kind, and exactly who she claims to be."
>
> —Scooter Braun via Instagram

got pregnant because she heard a rumor that Ari was pregnant.)

Matt Bennett: The pal and *Victorious* alum reprises *Bring It On*'s Cliff in the adorbs toothbrushing scene of the "Thank U, Next" video.

Scooter Braun: The man who discovered Justin Bieber has been Ari's manager since the beginning of her music career, and Ari describes him as a father figure.

Edward Butera: They've had a complicated relationship nearly all her life, but Ariana sees light even in the darkness. "I had to accept that it's okay not to get along with somebody and still love them," she told *Seventeen*.

Courtney Chipolone: Her hometown BFF did a pretty mean Gretchen from *Mean Girls* in the "Thank U, Next" video. That's fetch!

Miley Cyrus: She and Ari have plenty in common. They're both incredible vocalists and TV stars who have transitioned from their squeaky-clean, family-friendly images to come into their own as artists and women. Despite being pitted as rivals by fans and the media alike, they've long been supporters of each other's careers and causes, and have even dueted together.

Alfredo Flores: Best known for being Justin Bieber's bestie, Flores has served as Ari's tour photographer, sometime music video director, and documentarian behind the *Dangerous Woman Diaries*. Fredo even has his own legion of fans!

Kiyan Ghahreman: A familiar face in her entourage, Kiyan calls Ariana his "best friend and moonlight mother."

Backstage with Scooter Braun
on tour in 2017.

Elizabeth Gillies: These BFFs go way back. Ari met Liz while working on *13*, and they were then tapped to star on *Victorious* together. Gillies has gone on to work on various television and film projects and currently stars in the CW's *Dynasty* reboot.

Frank Grande: Ariana has called her maternal grandfather "my favorite person ever to exist." She was by his side in 2014 when he passed away from cancer. She even incorporated audio of Frank into her live performances: him saying "Don't let them challenge you. Don't let them intimidate you." Her tattoo *Bellissima* is a tribute to her grandfather, too.

Frankie Grande: Ariana's half-brother is talented in his own right! He's a singer-dancer-actor-model-TV host-YouTube personality and all-around supportive big brother who keeps his sis laughing.

Miley Cyrus and Ari onstage during the One Love Manchester benefit concert.

Walking the orange carpet with the Nicholson brothers at the 2013 Nickelodeon 10th Annual Worldwide Day of Play.

Joan Grande: Ariana's mom and all-around superwoman. Ariana once called her "the most badass, independent woman you'll ever meet," the person who taught her that "behind every successful woman is herself."

Marjorie Grande: Ariana's maternal grandmother, Nonna, is one of the central figures in her life. It was Nonna who encouraged Ariana to audition for *Annie*, Ariana's first major stage role. She's a constant source of inspiration, confidence, and humor in Ariana's life and a familiar face to Arianators. She's been onstage (like the time Ari brought up her mom, grandmother, and cousin to join her for a performance of "God Is a Woman" at the MTV Video Music Awards). Recently, she was Ariana's date when she won the huge honor of Billboard's Woman of the Year. Ari once described Nonna to her Instagram followers as "the epitome of style, grace, hilariousness, and badass Italian grandmotherness, the toughest of cookies and an inspiration to all." Now that's love!

Friendship reigns *Victorious!* Gillies, Aaron Simon Gross, and Grande in 2013.

Aaron Simon Gross: They met way back in their *13* days but have stayed close over the years. Keep an eye out—he often pops up on Ari's Instagram Stories.

Kaydence: A member of the "7 Rings" sorority, she cowrote "Rings" and "Thank U, Next," as well as "Better Off" from *Sweetener*.

Normani Kordei: Ari is tight with all the girls of Fifth Harmony, but it's Normani who will join Ari on her 2019 world tour.

Alexa Luria: A bestie from way back—the two met in elementary school!—influencer Luria runs the popular Instagram food/travel blog @girlwithagourmetpalate.

Doug Middlebrook: The Instragrammer and influencer extraordinaire is a good friend of Ari's, as well as her tour and production manager.

Nicki Minaj: Another so-called rival. Longtime musical collaborators (they've

> "[Ari] is one of the realest artists I've ever had the pleasure of working with."
> —Minaj to *Billboard*

done four singles together) Ari and Nicki have publicly stood by each other's side time and again—they even refer to each other as "big sis" and "little sis." Ari has mad respect for Nicki, calling her "one of the greatest rappers of all time, male or female" (*Paper* magazine).

Daniella Monet: Another friend from *Victorious*, she pops up as a TUN cheerleader in "Thank U, Next."

Victoria Monét: Ari's BFF is a singer/songwriter who has written tracks for everyone from Nas to Fifth Harmony to country singer Sara Evans. She's also cowritten tracks on every one of Ari's albums—three of them on *Thank U, Next*, including the title track. Monét calls Ari "a soul mate of a friend."

Brian and Scott Nicholson: Identical twins and backup dancers, they're both part of Ari's inner circle.

Njomza: A "7 Rings" bestie and collaborator, she is a musical artist in her own right.

Tayla Parx: A frequent collaborator with Ari, Parx is a songwriting wunderkind who has written for everyone from Mariah Carey to BTS to Pentatonix. She recently had *three* songs in the Billboard top 20 simultaneously, and her own debut album drops in 2019.

Troye Sivan: He tapped Ari to collaborate on his "Dance to This," but that didn't keep him from spreading some nasty gossip in the "Thank U, Next" video. IRL the pair has been tight for years. ♦

Performing "Better Days" with Victoria Monét at the One Love Manchester concert.

{7}

TATTOOED
HEART

"I have my things I love, I have my comfort zone."

Ariana has an unmistakable style that's all her own. From her signature top ponytail and cat's-eye eyeliner to her oversized sweatshirts and thigh-high boots to her multitude of tattoos, she slays.

Those tattoos are a front-and-center earmark of her style and a constantly evolving form of her self-expression.

She has about two dozen at last count, and she is constantly adding more. She brushes off the haters who think she'll regret some of those tats someday. "[They make] me so happy and I can't wait to be 90 and remember how happy my life was," she responded to a critic on Twitter.

When it comes to her hair, a lot of people don't know that her trademark ponytail was a case of form following function. Ari's natural hair is dark ("almost black") and curly, so to achieve the straight red locks she sported on *Victorious* and *Sam & Cat* took a lot of man-hours. And the end result was that Ari's hair became

{ *Parlor Games* }

After being named Billboard's Woman of the Year, Ariana celebrated in an unusual way. After the festivities she went straight to the tattoo parlor, where she got a crescent moon and stars inked on her hand. Oh, and Nonna got in on the action too. The 93-year-old had *Ciccio* tattooed on her finger in honor of her late husband. Ari posted footage of the occasion on her Instagram Story. "I feel fine. I've had more excitement than this," Nonna deadpanned to the camera.

so damaged and brittle from years of overprocessing that she ultimately ended up wearing a wig for her role of Cat Valentine. Once she left Nickelodeon, she couldn't go back to her natural locks. "My actual hair is so broken that it looks absolutely ratchet and absurd when I let it down," she told *US* magazine in 2014. Rather than continue wearing wigs, a look she called "RIDICULOUS," she opted for extensions. And she's been rocking them ever since.

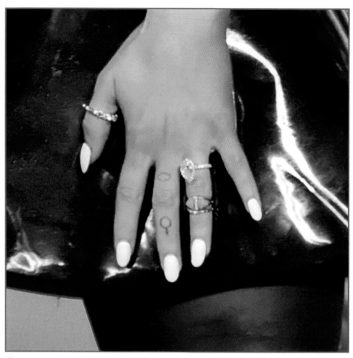

If you can see past the bling, you'll catch Ari's cloud and female symbol tattoos.

Another mainstay over the years—and what many petite women might consider a necessity—are the sky-high heels Ari is always sporting. At five foot zero, Ari is more accomplished at wearing six-inch heels than most runway models. "I think there's something wrong with me, for sure," she told *Footwear News*. "If you wanted me to I could, like, run."

Ari's stylist, Law Roach, seconds that, offering this "high" praise of Ari to *ELLE*: "I've worked with a lot of women, and been around a lot of women, but I have never met anyone who can wear high-heeled shoes like her. Never. She walks around in platform shoes all day long…. I always call her Magic Feet. I've never seen anything like it, ever."

{ "I always call her Magic Feet. I've never seen anything like it, ever." }

Audrey Hepburn
meets Minnie in 2014.

Ari calls the Vera Wang dress she wore to the 2018 Met Gala "the puff puff dream."

Ariana's fashion evolution has been dramatic. An early style icon was Audrey Hepburn, and Ari has channeled the actress and humanitarian's demure style beautifully. As she evolved as an artist, so has her style. Fifties glam is a far cry from the big hoodies and stiletto boots she rocks these days (a difficult-to-pull-off look *ELLE* dubbed "lampshading").

"I have my things I love, I have my comfort zone," Ari told *Paper.* "I think that fashion should be more of a self-expression thing as opposed to a trend thing. To me, when I feel really dope and I have an outfit on that makes me really happy, that's so much better." And maybe that's why she's become such a fashion icon, because her style comes from the inside out.

MTV News rhapsodized about the diva's sartorial choices, saying, "[S]he's boasted floor-length red gowns, chokers, crop tops, and oversize jackets [and] everything from theater garb…to Mickey

> ### { *$45 million* }
>
> According to the website Celebrity Net Worth, Ari is worth an estimated $45 million. The singer made an estimated *$50,000 a day* on merchandise sales alone during her last tour. That's a lot of oversized sweatshirts!

Mouse ears to A-line minis. Which, in an industry rich in self-branding, is a beautiful rarity…. [D]ismissing Ariana Grande as a fashion force is an easy and lazy way of categorizing her…. [F]ashion is best when it's an extension of self and a wearable form of expression. (Plus, we know that when we see someone take risks, they understand fashion on an intrinsic level.)"

Love it or hate it, one thing is for certain: Ari's style is never, ever boring. ♦

{ *Ari's Tattoos: A Field Guide* }

Since she's always adding—and sometimes editing—the following is an exhaustive, if not complete, guide to Ariana's tattoos.

אלד: These Hebrew characters reference one of the 72 names of God.

561: The area code of Boca Raton, her hometown.

7 Rings: Ari's infamous barbecue grill tattoo has been corrected and now reads 7 RINGS.

8418: Another bygone tattoo, this was the badge number of Pete Davidson's late dad, a firefighter and 9/11 first responder.

A: Located on her thumb, this is a shout-out to bestie Alexa Luria.

Always: Fans have speculated that this is a nod to the Harry Potter series, among Ari's favorites. It's one of the book series' most famous—and romantic—lines.

Baby Doll: A nickname given to Ari by her family, this one is located on her finger.

Bee: A symbol of the city of Manchester, Ari got this in remembrance of the tragedy.

Bellissima: "Beautiful" in Italian, this is a tribute to her late grandfather. "It's the name he called me my whole life," she tweeted.

Black heart: This matches one her ex Davidson has.

Chihiro Ogino: Heroine of the animated film *Spirited Away*, Ari explained the character's significance in an Instagram Story. "She matures from an easily scared girl with a childlike personality to match her age to a hardworking, responsible, and brave young girl who has learned to put her fears aside for those she cares for."

Cloud: Another finger tattoo, this was reportedly the inspiration for her eponymous perfume.

Crescent moon: Located on her neck, this might be a nod to her song "Moonlight."

Crescent moon and stars: Designed by Brooklyn tattoo artist Mira Mariah, a frequent collaborator, she added this one the night Nonna got inked!

Eevee: Ari's got mad love for this Pokémon character.

H2GKMO: Celebrating one of Ariana's favorite sayings—"Honest to God, knock me out."

Heart outline: Another toe embellishment.

Hi: Because she thought her toe wasn't friendly enough?

Honeymoon: Another finger tattoo, this one may be a nod to her first tour, the Honeymoon tour.

Let's sing: She added this phrase, in Japanese characters, to her inner arm.

Lightning bolt: Another potential nod to Harry Potter, and the hero's signature lightning bolt scar.

Lumos: Yet another Potter tattoo, this references the spell that creates light in the darkness.

Mille tendresse: Translated from the French as "a thousand tendernesses," the tattoo is a nod to *Breakfast at Tiffany's*, a favorite film.

Myron: After Mac Miller's death, Ari reportedly adopted his dog, Myron. Eagle-eyed fans spotted the new ink in her "Thank U, Next" video; it covers up a previous tattoo she got in memory of ex-fiancé Pete Davidson's late father.

Olive branch: Another tattoo covering up previous ink, she turned a matching tattoo she'd gotten with Pete Davidson into the ultimate symbol of peace. "I have no words to describe how much I love and am eternally grateful for these human beings who constantly help me turn lemons into lemonade and literally heal me and put me back together," she wrote on Instagram about the new tattoo.

Pete: She got this one tattooed on her ring finger after her engagement to the comedian. It's since been covered up.

Reborn: Yet another matching tattoo she got with Pete Davidson.

REM: Located behind her right ear, fans first spotted this in her "Breathin" video.

Venus symbol: Symbolizing the female, she got this one on her finger.

{8}

NO TEARS
LEFT TO CRY

Riding high on the success of her Dangerous Woman tour, Ariana arrived in Manchester, England, to play to a packed stadium of fans on May 22, 2017.

Then the unthinkable happened. As the performance was ending and the crowd began to leave the arena, a suicide bomber detonated a homemade explosive device just outside the venue. Twenty-two people, including young children, were killed; hundreds more were injured.

It was the most devastating terrorist attack on British soil in more than a decade, and it was personally devastating to Ari, who was weighed down heavily with guilt. "Broken," she wrote to her fans on Twitter. "From the bottom of my heart, I am so sorry. I don't have words."

Performing with the Parrs Wood High School choir.

More than 50,000 people strong.

She canceled her upcoming tour dates and returned home, utterly distraught and unsure if she would ever sing again. She was unreachable for days, barely speaking and sobbing endlessly. "Then Joan got a knock on her door," *ELLE* reported. "'It was two or three in the morning,' Joan remembered. '[Ari] crawled into bed and said, "Mom, let's be honest, I'm never not going to sing again. But I'm not going to sing again until I sing in Manchester first."'"

She called her manager, Scooter Braun, the *Wall Street Journal* reported. "I've been thinking a lot, and if we don't do something, everyone will have died in vain," she told him. From that conversation, the One Love Manchester benefit took seed. They agreed that they wanted to do it as soon as possible, to take an immediate stand against the hate. They invited the families of the victims and gathered an impressive roster of performers in short order.

The concert was held on June 4—less than two weeks after the attack—and raised $13 million for the We Love Manchester Emergency Fund. More than 14,000 ticket holders from the May 22 concert were in attendance. Among the artists who appeared in support of the cause were Coldplay, Stevie Wonder, Miley Cyrus, Katy Perry, Justin Bieber, Robbie Williams, Take That, Niall Horan, the Black Eyed Peas, Pharrell Williams, Mac Miller, Imogen Heap, Marcus Mumford, and Oasis' Liam Gallagher. (Additional artists appeared remotely, including U2,

Coldplay delights the crowd.

> "Grande burns bright as a symbol of resilience: a young woman who defied the belittling diva narrative; who says she emerged from tragedy 'loving a bit more fearlessly' than she did before."
> —The *Guardian*

Paul McCartney, Sam Smith, Jennifer Hudson, Chance the Rapper, Halsey, Demi Lovato, Rita Ora, Shawn Mendes, and Camila Cabello, among others.)

"They're trying to make us scared and make us live in fear, and we can't play into their hands," Ariana told the crowd during the benefit. "They want us to hate each other and cross-divide communities and we can't, we can't let that happen. We can't do that." And in the face of fear and still reeling from grief, Manchester indeed stood united.

The One Love Manchester concert was broadcast on dozens of radio stations around the world in addition to being livestreamed for millions of viewers and listeners. *New York Magazine* called it the best concert of the year, writing:

After meeting with a parent of one of the victims, Grande said she shifted the tone of the show from somber to celebratory because she understood that it was what her fans needed. But could she make them smile again? From the moment she strutted onstage in stilettos and a hoodie with a crew of voguing dancers to "Be Alright," the entire crowd knew they would be. All night, Ariana performed without breaking, but that was when she had others by her side to calm her nerves.... When it was just her alone with her fans for her finale cover of "Somewhere Over the Rainbow," the floodgates opened. In what will likely go down as one of the defining moments of her career, she paused the song, looked out to her audience, which was already sobbing along with her, then resumed the music to nail yet another impossible note.

Ari later admitted to being terrified to return to the stage but credits the fans with lifting her back up. "Why would I second-guess getting on a…stage and being there for them? That city, and their response? That changed my life," she told *ELLE* in 2018.

She has also opened up about the crippling effects of anxiety attacks and PTSD she has suffered since the tragedy, and revealed that she has been in therapy for more than a decade. "Therapy has saved my life so many times," she tweeted. "if you're afraid to ask for help,

Justin Bieber performs for Manchester.

don't be. u don't have to be in constant pain & u can process trauma. i've got a lot of work to do but it's a start to even be aware that it's possible." By shining a light on her own struggles, she's helped countless fans through their own difficulties—a refrain Arianators repeat time and again.

Ari's first order of business after wrapping the Dangerous Woman tour was to head back into the studio, and she emerged with a powerful song about Manchester, the first music she released since the tragedy. "No Tears Left to Cry" was the ultimate catharsis after a very arduous span of months.

The events of Manchester tinge *Sweetener* from its opening track, "Raindrops (An Angel Cried)," to the end—the last song ends with 40 seconds of silence, making it exactly 5:22, the date of the attack. But beyond that, Ari emerges as an artist reborn and self-assured.

Manchester put Ari's bigheartedness on full display, but it's far from the only time she's devoted herself to raising money and awareness for a needful cause. Ari appeared on DoSomething.org's 2018 list of most charitable celebrities. (That's pretty impressive, especially when you consider that, according to the *Wall Street Journal*, "Braun stipulates that every deal for a client include some sort of charitable component and encourages clients to donate the way he does: '50 percent quiet charity—you say nothing—and 50 percent that you show.'")

Among the many charities that she's given her time and money to are PETA, the Make-A-Wish Foundation, and various cancer research organizations.

"We just have to be there for each other as much as we can," Ari told Beats 1 Radio. And she seems to be one artist who's doing just that. ♦

Ari leaves the stage in tears.

"There's not much I'm afraid of anymore."
—to *Billboard* in 2018

{The Medicine the World Needs Right Now}

From Marcus Mumford's opening moment of silence to Ari's last Judy Garland–inspired note, the One Love Manchester concert was outstanding. Here's the setlist from the epic show.

Marcus Mumford, "Timshel"

Take That, "Shine"

Take That, "Giants"

Take That, "Rule the World"

Robbie Williams, "Strong (Manchester We're Strong)"

Robbie Williams, "Angels"

Pharrell Williams, "Get Lucky"

Pharrell Williams and Miley Cyrus, "Happy"

Miley Cyrus, "Inspired"

Niall Horan, "Slow Hands"

Niall Horan, "This Town"

Ariana Grande, "Be Alright"

Ariana Grande, "Break Free"

Stevie Wonder, "Love's in Need of Love Today"

Little Mix, "Wings"

Ariana Grande and Victoria Monét, "Better Days"

The Black Eyed Peas and Ariana Grande, "Where Is the Love?"

Imogen Heap, "Hide and Seek"

Ariana Grande and Parrs Wood High School Choir, "My Everything"

Ariana Grande and Mac Miller, "The Way"

Ariana Grande and Mac Miller, "Dang!"

Ariana Grande and Miley Cyrus, "Don't Dream It's Over"

Ariana Grande, "Side to Side"

Katy Perry, "Part of Me"

Katy Perry, "Roar"

Justin Bieber, "Love Yourself"

Justin Bieber, "Cold Water"

Ariana Grande, "Love Me Harder"

Ariana Grande and Coldplay, "Don't Look Back in Anger"

Coldplay, "Fix You"

Coldplay, "Viva la Vida"

Coldplay, "Something Just Like This"

Liam Gallagher, "Rock 'n' Roll Star"

Liam Gallagher, "Wall of Glass"

Liam Gallagher and Coldplay, "Live Forever"

All Artists, "One Last Time"

Ariana Grande, "Somewhere Over the Rainbow"

{9}

THANK U, NEXT

For all of the success and attention that Ari has received because of her music, sometimes it seems as if she's received even more attention for her personal life.

No more was that put into laser focus than during her short-lived engagement to Pete Davidson. Tabloids and respectable news outlets alike blared headlines about the pair seemingly every day. Wasn't it just a rebound? (Pete had just split from long-term girlfriend Cazzie David and Ari had ended things with Mac Miller months earlier.) Was the engagement way too much too soon? And what about all those matching tattoos? Surely *those* were a mistake.

Of course, the honeymoon was over before it even began, and by October 2018 Ari was left grieving not only her broken engagement but the death of Miller. "Remember when i was like hey i have no tears left to cry and the universe was like HAAAAAAAA…u thought," she tweeted. She went straight into the studio with her inner circle of friends, working feverishly and channeling her emotions into the collection of songs that became *Thank U, Next*. Through that process, she began the long and difficult process of healing.

Despite how rough things were for her, she had an incredible amount of perspective early on. Speaking to *Billboard* in November 2018, she had this to say about Davidson: "This is how I meet people—I can't just, like, meet someone at a bar. I live fast and full-out, and I make mistakes, and I learn from them and I'm grateful no matter what happens." Statements like that one shed a lot of light on "Thank U, Next" and its ethos.

Cowriter Victoria Monét expanded on the concept, tweeting the directive "learn to say Thank u, next": "Not everything is supposed to be long-lasting. Sometimes

"Wish I could say 'thank you' to Malcolm / 'Cause he was an angel."

The artist at the top of her game.

{ *33* }

"Thank U, Next" was only the 32nd song in the Billboard Hot 100's 70-year history to make its chart debut at No. 1. "7 Rings" became lucky 33 when it topped the charts in February 2019.

people come into your life to show you what is right and what is wrong, to show you who you can be, to teach you to love yourself, to make you feel better for a little while, or just to be someone to walk with at night and spill your life to. Not everyone is going to stay forever, and we still have to keep on going and thank them for what they've given us."

The release of the single had immediate impact. With absolutely no promotion or lead-up, it debuted at the top of the charts—Ari's first No. 1 single ever—busted streaming records, and inspired a gazillion memes and imitations. Holding the No. 1 position on the Billboard Hot 100 for eight straight weeks, "Thank U, Next" is nothing short of a phenomenon.

While self-empowerment may be the focus of the title single, the release of "Imagine" shows another side of the coin altogether. Responding to a fan on Twitter asking for details on the fifth album, Ari wrote, "a lot of this album mourns failed yet important, beautiful relationships in my life (as well as celebrates growth / exploring new independence). but for those of you asking about imagine: i would say if

'thank u, next' = acceptance... 'imagine' = denial." Fans have speculated that "Imagine" was written about Miller, and it's a beautiful alternate reality to imagine indeed.

Ari scored a trifecta with "7 Rings," the record's third single. A very different take on the theme of self-care, it's an unapologetic ode to retail therapy and being an all-around boss. The song obliterated streaming records and skyrocketed to the top of the charts, positioning Thank U, Next for an absolutely huge album release. ♦

{ *Three's Company* }

Just four days after the release of "Thank U, Next," Ari appeared on *Ellen* with friends and cowriters Tayla Parx and Victoria Monét to perform the song. Clad in all white, the trio channeled the iconic final scene in *The First Wives Club*, when Bette Midler, Diane Keaton, and Goldie Hawn's characters make their own declaration of independence, performing an impromptu version of Lesley Gore's "You Don't Own Me."

Ari is ready to be the
reigning Queen of Pop.

{Easter Egg Hunting in the "Thank U, Next" Video}

Ari is no stranger to hiding Easter eggs in her videos. She likes to tease titles and lyrics for upcoming releases on the regular. But "Thank U, Next" is next-level. Besides re-creating some of the most beloved scenes from *Mean Girls*, *13 Going on 30*, *Bring It On*, and *Legally Blonde*, she also manages to interweave a ton of goodies for Arianators into it.

For starters, Ari brings some of the best scenes from the rom-coms to life, including Elle Woods' "bend and snap," Karen Smith's uncanny weather skills, the heartbreaking dollhouse scene from *13 Going on 30*, and the awkwardly cute toothbrushing scene from *Bring It On*.

The video is also chock-full of inspired casting. First, a cavalcade of Ari's friends, including Alexa Luria, Courtney Chipolone, Victoria Monét, Tayla Parx, Liz Gillies, Troye Sivan…the list goes on! Then there's uber-mom Kris Jenner reprising the role of Amy Poehler's cool mom in *Mean Girls*. And actors Jennifer Coolidge (Paulette!), Jonathan Bennett (Aaron Samuels!), and Stefanie Drummond reprise their original film roles. Ariana lookalike Gabi DeMartino also stars, wearing a "Babygirl" (Arianators' nickname for their idol) T-shirt. Oh, and did I mention that Ari's real-life dog Toulouse takes over for *Legally Blonde*'s Bruiser?

The *Mean Girls*–inspired burn book is bursting with references, including an open invitation or two and some very personal information about one of her exes. In case you missed it, the courier sports a uniform that's a very specific reference to ex Pete Davidson.

Almost each scene has "Thank U, Next" embedded somewhere in it, from signs on the wall to the TUN cheerleaders in the *Bring It On*–inspired segment.

Ari revealed via Twitter that there's a framed photo of Mac Miller on the nightstand next to "Regina's" bed. There's also a framed pic of Joan and Nonna on Paulette's manicure station and photos of Nonna and Frank Grande in "Elle's" dorm room. And a poster of brother Frankie hangs in Ari's Regina George bedroom.

There are at least three references to future singles: the 7 RINGS vanity license plate and IMAGINE, which is emblazoned on the bleachers during a *Bring It On* scene. Ari's Regina shirt reads A LITTLE BIT NEEDY.

Jonathan Bennett carries his real-life *Mean Girls*–inspired cookbook through the halls in the video. And of course there's the aforementioned dig on the commander in chief.

The attention to detail is next-level. Check the dollhouse in the *13 Going on 30* sequence—each room is a miniature of the sets seen throughout the video! A miniature of Ari—sans extensions (a Snapchat pic that previously set the Internet afire)—sits in the bathtub.

Above all, the mixtape, *From Ari to Ari*—which is presumably the full album *Thank U, Next*—is the ultimate catharsis for Ari in the video, just as it was for Torrance in *Bring It On*. And in reality, it gets Arianators hyped up to hear the rest!

Onstage during the Sweetener Sessions in 2018.

{10}

IMAGINE

After everything that's happened in her already wildly successful career, it's hard to imagine what's in store for Ari. But let's start with what's on tap in 2019. She entered the New Year with a seventh-straight week at No. 1 on the charts with "Thank U, Next." She slipped off the No. 1 spot for just three before she came storming back, with "7 Rings" recapturing the top spot on the charts in its debut week.

She embarks on a world tour in support of not one but two albums in *Sweetener* and *Thank U, Next* in March. Dates are being added by popular demand, as shows are already selling out in cities across the globe.

And she'll make history as the headliner for the uber-popular Coachella festival—the youngest female headliner in the venerable concert's history. Unbelievably, she's only the fourth female artist to headline the show (following Beyoncé, Lady Gaga, and Björk—good company!). She'll also reportedly be headlining Lollapalooza, for good measure.

All the while, she'll be working on even more music. "Social House is my opening act [on tour]," she told *Billboard*. "You don't think we're going to have a studio on the bus? That we're not going to be making records on the road? Of course we are," she revealed.

Just don't ask her about her love life. It's about the music, remember? She's already announced that she's not dating for the rest of this year, and possibly not ever again. And even though that may be tongue in cheek, it's a shrewd move from Ari, who has constantly tried to keep the focus on the music, even in the face of inane questions from the media about makeup and high heels and relentless speculation about her personal life.

Her relentless work ethic and focus is bearing fruit. By all counts, it seems assured that 2019 will be the year of Ari. And for that, Arianators may rejoice! ◆

Ari is poised for a long
career in the limelight.

"I feel like I've only scratched the surface of the artist I can be."